AMAZING ANIMALS
OF THE WORLD ②

Volume 4

Frog, Burrowing Tree — Guenon, Moustached

GROLIER

First published 2005 by Grolier, an imprint of Scholastic Library Publishing

For information address the publisher: Grolier, Scholastic Library Publishing
90 Old Sherman Turnpike
Danbury, CT 06816

Set ISBN: 0-7172-6112-3; Volume ISBN: 0-7172-6116-6

Printed and bound in the U.S.A.

Library of Congress Cataloging-in-Publications Data:
Amazing animals of the world 2.
p.cm.
Includes indexes.
Contents: v. 1. Adder—Buffalo, Water -- v. 2. Bunting, Corn—Cricket, Bush -- v. 3. Cricket, European Mole—Frog, Agile -- v. 4. Frog, Burrowing Tree—Guenon, Moustached -- v. 5. Gull, Great Black-backed—Loach, Stone -- v. 6. Locust, Migratory—Newt, Crested -- v. 7. Nuthatch, Eurasian—Razor, Pod -- v. 8. Reedbuck, Mountain—Snake, Tentacled -- v. 9. Snakefly—Toad, Surinam -- v. 10. Tortoise, Gopher—Zebu.
ISBN 0-7172-6112-3 (set : alk. paper) -- ISBN 0-7172-6113-1 (v. 1 : alk. paper) -- ISBN 0-7172-6114-X (v. 2 : alk. paper) -- ISBN 0-7172-6115-8 (v. 3 : alk. paper) -- ISBN 0-7172-6116-6 (v. 4 : alk. paper) -- ISBN 0-7172-6117-4 (v. 5 : alk. paper) -- ISBN 0-7172-6118-2 (v. 6 : alk. paper) -- ISBN 0-7172-6119-0 (v. 7 : alk. paper) -- ISBN 0-7172-6120-4 (v. 8 : alk. paper) -- ISBN 0-7172-6121-2 (v. 9 : alk. paper) -- ISBN 0-7172-6122-0 (v. 10 : alk.paper)
1. Animals--Juvenile literature. I. Title: Amazing animals of the world two. II. Grolier (Firm)
QL49.A455 2005
590--dc22
2005040351

About This Set

Amazing Animals of the World 2 brings you pictures of 400 fascinating creatures and important information about how and where they live.

Each page shows just one species—individual type—of animal. They all fall into seven main categories or groups of animals (classes and phylums scientifically) that appear on each page as an icon or picture—amphibians, arthropods, birds, fish, mammals, other invertebrates, and reptiles. Short explanations of what these group names mean, and other terms used commonly in the set, appear on page 4 in the Glossary.

Scientists use all kinds of groupings to help them sort out the thousands of types of animals that exist today and once wandered here (extinct species). Kingdoms, classes, phylums, genus, and species are among the key words here that are also explained in the Glossary (page 4).

Where animals live is important to know as well. Each of the species in this set lives in a particular place in the world, which you can see outlined on the map on each page. And in those locales the animals tend to favor a particular habitat—an environment the animal finds suitable for life, with food, shelter, and safety from predators that might eat it. There they also find ways to coexist with other animals in the area that might eat somewhat different food, use different homes, and so on. Each of the main habitats is named on the page and given an icon/picture to help you envision it. The habitat names are further defined in the Glossary on page 4.

As well as being part of groups like species, animals fall into other categories that help us understand their lives or behavior. You will find these categories in the Glossary on page 4, where you will learn about carnivores, herbivores, and other types of animals.

And there is more information you might want about an animal—its size, diet, where it lives, and how it carries on its species—the way it creates its young. All these facts and more appear in the data boxes at the top of each page.

Finally, you should know that the set is arranged alphabetically by the most common name of the species. That puts most beetles, say, together in a group so you can compare them easily.

But some animals' names are not so common, and they don't appear near others like them. For instance, the chamois is a kind of goat or antelope. To find animals that are similar—or to locate any species—look in the index at the end of each book in the set (pages 45-48). It lists all animals by their various names (you will find the giant South American river turtle under turtle, giant South American river, and also under its other name—arrau). And you will find all birds, fish, and so on gathered under their broader groupings.

Similarly, smaller like groups appear in the set index as well—butterflies include swallowtails and blues, for example.

Table of Contents
Volume 4

Glossary

Amphibians—species usually born from eggs in water or wet places, which change (metamorphose) into a land animal. Frogs and salamanders are typical. They breathe through their skin mainly and have no scales.

Arctic and Antarctic—icy, cold, dry areas at the ends of the globe that lack trees but see small plants grown in thawed areas (tundra). Penguins and seals are common inhabitants.

Arthropods—animals with segmented bodies, hard outer skin, and jointed legs, such as spiders and crabs.

Birds—born from eggs, these creatures have wings and often can fly. Eagles, pigeons, and penguins are all birds, though penguins can't fly through the air.

Carnivores—they are animals that eat other animals. Many species do eat each other sometimes, and a few eat dead animals. Lions kill their prey and eat it, while vultures clean up dead bodies of animals.

Cities, Towns, and Farms—places where people live and have built or used the land and share it with many species. Sometimes these animals live in human homes or just nearby.

Class—part or division of a phylum.

Deserts—dry, often warm areas where animals often are more active on cooler nights or near water sources. Owls, scorpions, and jack rabbits are common in American deserts.

Endangered—some animals in this set are marked as endangered because it is possible they will become extinct soon.

Extinct—these species have died out altogether for whatever reason.

Family—part of an order.

Fish—water animals (aquatic) that typically are born from eggs and breathe through gills. Trout and eels are fish, though whales and dolphins are not (they are mammals).

Forests and Mountains—places where evergreen (coniferous) and leaf-shedding (deciduous) trees are common, or that rise in elevation to make cool, separate habitats. **Rainforests are different (see below).**

Fresh Water—lakes, rivers, and the like carry fresh water (unlike Oceans and Shores, where the water is salty). Fish and birds abound, as do insects, frogs, and mammals.

Genus—part of a family.

Grasslands—habitats with few trees and light rainfall. Grasslands often lie between forests and deserts, and they are home to birds, coyotes, antelope, and snakes, as well as many other kinds of animals.

Herbivores—these animals eat mainly plants. Typical are hoofed animals (ungulates) that are common on grasslands, such as antelope or deer. Domestic (nonwild) ones are cows and horses.

Hibernators—species that live in harsh areas with very cold winters slow down their functions then and sort of sleep through the hard times.

Kingdom—the largest division of species. Commonly there are understood to be five kingdoms: animals, plants, fungi, protists, and monerans.

Mammals—these creatures usually bear live young and feed them on milk from the mother. A few lay eggs (monotremes like the platypus) or nurse young in a pouch (marsupials like opossums and kangaroos).

Migrators—some species spend different seasons in different places, moving to where more food, warmth, or safety can be found. Birds often do this, sometimes over long distances, but others types of animals also move seasonally, including fish and mammals.

Oceans and Shores—seawater is salty, often deep, and huge. In it live many fish, invertebrates, and even some mammals, such as whales. On the shore birds and other creatures often gather.

Order—part of a class.

Other Invertebrates—animals that lack backbones or internal skeletons. Many, such as insects and shrimp, have hard outer coverings. Clams and worms are also invertebrates.

Phylum—part of a kingdom.

Rainforests—here huge trees grow among many other plants helped by the warm, wet environment. Thousands of species of animals also live in these rich habitats.

Reptiles—these species have scales, lungs to breathe, and lay eggs or give birth to live young. Dinosaurs are thought to have been reptiles, while today the class includes turtles, snakes, lizards, and crocodiles.

Scientific name—the genus and species name of a creature in Latin. For instance, Canis lupus is the wolf. Scientific names avoid the confusion possible with common names in any one language or across languages.

Species—a group of the same type of living thing. Part of an order.

Subspecies—a variant but quite similar part of a species.

Territorial—many animals mark out and defend a patch of ground as their home area. Birds and mammals may call quite small or quite large spots their territories.

Vertebrates—animals with backbones and skeletons under their skins

Burrowing Tree Frog
Pternohyla fodiens

Length: 1 to 2 inches
Diet: insects and small invertebrates
Method of Reproduction: egg layer

Home: southern Arizona and Mexico
Order: Frogs and toads
Family: Tree frogs and their relatives

 Grasslands

 Amphibians

© TOM MCHUGH / PHOTO RESEARCHERS

Most tree frogs live far off the ground, clinging to damp vegetation with their sticky toe pads. Over the years a few species—such as the burrowing tree frog—have evolved into ground dwellers and have lost their suction-cup toes. Like many burrowing toads, this tree frog digs itself into the earth using spadelike horns on its back legs. By seeking underground shelter from the sun, the tree frog is able to survive in dry grasslands and mesquite woods.

The skin on the burrowing tree frog's head is tightly attached to a very hard, broad skull. Biologists think that this bony helmet makes a strong stopper for the top of the tree frog's burrow. By plugging its damp hole, the frog can slow the loss of moisture from its body. Its helmet may also protect the buried frog from the teeth of predators.

Burrowing tree frogs leave their burrows on rainy and damp nights. They breed in July and August, when summer rains form puddles and temporary ponds. At dusk the breeding males gather in the water to call for their mates with deep, loud squawks. Normally shy and easily frightened, the chorusing frogs become totally engrossed in their singing. As a result, they are easily caught by both humans and animal predators. After mating in the shallow water, the females lay jellylike clumps of eggs. The hatching tadpoles must develop quickly and transform into adult frogs before their ponds evaporate under the hot sun.

Common Gray Tree Frog
Hyla versicolor

Length: 1¼ to 2½ inches
Method of Reproduction: egg layer
Home: central and eastern North America

Diet: mainly insects
Order: Frogs and toads
Family: Tree frogs and their relatives

 Fresh Water

Amphibians

© JOHN SERRAO / PHOTO RESEARCHERS

The common gray tree frog sounds a familiar call on spring and summer evenings throughout much of North America. Its loud song echoes through the night like the trilling of a whistle. While the majority of tree frogs are slender, the gray tree frog is rather stout, almost toadlike in appearance. Its warty skin also resembles that of a toad.

Despite its name, the gray tree frog is just as likely to be green or brown. It is best recognized by the distinctive light-colored patch beneath each eye. Its back is marked with large, dark blotches and lines, and the insides of its thighs are a yellowish orange.

Common gray tree frogs live in low trees and shrubs near lakes and streams. The male is especially fond of branches that hang over shallow water. From such a perch, he calls through the night. When a female draws near, the male joins her in the water. Approaching from behind, he grasps her around the chest. This signals the female to lay a mass of eggs, which he fertilizes.

In appearance the common gray tree frog is identical to Cope's gray tree frog, *H. chrysoscelis*, which shares its range. Cope's gray sings with a somewhat faster trill. But the only reliable way to distinguish the two species is by examining their cells with a powerful microscope. The cells of the common gray tree frog contain twice as many chromosomes as do the Cope's.

European Tree Frog
Hyla arborea

Length: 1 to 2 inches
Diet: mainly insects
Method of Reproduction: egg layer

Home: Europe
Order: Frogs and toads
Family: Tree frogs and their relatives

Fresh Water

Amphibians

© MICHAEL GORE / FRANK LANE PICTURE AGENCY / CORBIS

The fact that the European tree frog is a plump little creature doesn't keep it from doing some amazing things. For starters, the frog can adhere to leaves and tree bark, thanks to loose skin on its belly that acts like a rubber suction cup. Using its suction-cup feet, a European tree frog can climb even the slipperiest surfaces. With this ability, the frog can use most any surface as a launching pad from which to leap into the air and swallow a flying insect in midflight!

The European tree frog also has the unusual ability to change color according to the weather. On sunny days, it turns bright green. When clouds move in, the frog fades to a grayish green. Such color changes help the frog go undetected by predators until it moves. Then, if frightened, the frog changes color again, usually to a vivid green.

In spring, European tree frogs gather at ponds to mate and lay eggs. During the day, they sit in the sun on thin plant stems along the shore or over the water. As night begins to fall, the males descend to the water's surface and begin to call, making a "keck-keck-keck" sound 6 to 10 times in a row. The calls attract female tree frogs. During mating, the females lay small clumps of eggs that are immediately fertilized by the males. The females then use their hind legs to attach the eggs to plants in the water. The eggs hatch into tadpoles. By midsummer the tadpoles metamorphose, or change, into small tree frogs.

Gold Frog
Mantella aurantiaca

Length: ¾ to 1 inch
Diet: insects
Method of Reproduction: egg layer

Home: Madagascar
Order: Frogs and toads
Family: Old World tree frogs

 Rainforests

 Amphibians

© DAVID A. NORTHCOTT / CORBIS

Some say the gold frog is the most beautiful frog in the world. As a result, thousands are sold each year to people who fancy them as terrarium pets. They are not a good investment, however. Gold frogs are delicate creatures that do not live a long life when they are away from their rainforest home.

Scientists know little about the gold frog. The female of most frog species releases eggs in water, where they are fertilized by sperm from a male. But as far as biologists can tell, the male gold frog fertilizes the female's eggs while they are still inside her body. After the eggs have grown to a large size, she then deposits them on the ground instead of in the water. Biologists have never seen a gold frog tadpole and believe that the young may hatch as tiny frogs.

The gold frog lives deep within the rainforests of Madagascar. It is not officially listed as endangered because no one knows just how many there are. But it is surely in big trouble, according to experts, because its home is being destroyed. One of the reasons that people make such a fuss about the destruction of rainforests is because these forests are home to more animals than can be counted. As is the case with the gold frog, we know very little about many of these tropical animals. The danger is that they will disappear before we have a chance to learn about their wonderful ways.

Marbled Reed Frog
Hyperolius marmoratus

Length: ¾ to 1½ inches
Diet: insects and other small invertebrates
Method of Reproduction: egg layer

Home: Tanzania and southern Kenya
Order: Frogs and toads
Family: Rhacophorids

 Fresh Water

 Amphibians

When a young marbled reed frog first leaves the water (having just transformed from a tadpole into an adult), its skin is a drab brown. Over the next few months, a dramatic color transformation takes place: the skin lightens to a creamy shade of white, gray, or pink, and the frog develops dark streaks and spots on its head, back, and legs. Such intense color and pattern changes are unusual for frogs. Most young frogs are exact replicas of their parents. The brown skin of the immature reed frog helps it hide from predators. The bolder markings of the mature frogs help them recognize each other during the mating season.

Marbled reed frogs are known as "winter frogs" because they are rarely seen except during the cool-weather breeding season. During the summer, these frogs stay hidden in thick grasses and reeds, and emerge only at night. They are excellent climbers, thanks to the suction cups on their long, slender back toes. The cups help the frog adhere to reeds and grasses.

As the weather cools, marbled reed frogs become less shy. By winter, many hunt throughout the day near the edges of swamps and pools. They also become bold about mating and laying eggs in full view of humans and predators. After the breeding season, the frogs seem to suddenly vanish. Left behind are jellylike masses of eggs and wriggling tadpoles.

Marsupial Frog
Gastrotheca marsupiata

Length: up to 1½ inches
Number of Eggs: about 200
Method of Reproduction: egg layer

Diet: insects
Home: Ecuador and Peru
Order: Frogs and toads
Family: Tree frogs

 Rainforests

 Amphibians

© DAVID A. NORTHCOTT / CORBIS

The marsupial frog's scientific genus name, *Gastrotheca*, means "belly container." That gives you a hint about how this frog cares for its young. Like the kangaroo and other marsupials, the female of this frog species carries her newborn babies in a pouch until they are old enough to enter the outside world.

Actually, the name "belly container" is misleading. The female frog's pouch is on her back. When the frogs mate, the small male climbs onto the larger female frog's back. He fertilizes each of her eggs as they come out of her body. Then he packs them into the pouch and closes the flap over them.

Over the next few weeks, the eggs develop into tadpoles. The mother then finds a pond or puddle suitable for her babies. To release them, she reaches up over her back with a hind leg and slits open the pouch with her longest toe. The tadpoles them tumble out into the water to begin life on their own.

Some subspecies of marsupial frogs keep their young inside their pouches until they develop completely—from eggs to tadpoles to tiny adult frogs. In these frogs, each tadpole has a yolk sac that provides food during its time inside the mother's pouch. These frogs lay only one-tenth as many eggs as other marsupial frogs. But each baby has a better chance of survival because it is more developed when it finally enters the dangerous outside world.

Moor Frog
Rana arvalis

Length: 2¼ to 3 inches
Diet: insects, worms, and other invertebrates
Method of Reproduction: egg layer

Home: northern and central Europe and western Asia
Order: Frogs and toads
Family: Common frogs

 Fresh Water

 Amphibians

© OLEG KOSTERIN / BRUCE COLEMAN INC.

The moor frog is well suited to receive the title "periscope of the animal kingdom." With eyes set high on its head, the moor frog can glide through the water with only its eyes above the surface— much like the periscope of a submerged submarine. In this way the moor frog eludes its most common predators—snakes, storks, herons, foxes, polecats, and otters.

The moor frog, in turn, has a hearty appetite of its own. In its favorite habitat— lakes and ponds in wet, boggy moors—the moor frog uses its keen vision to spot a moving insect or other prey. Then, in a split second, it flips out its tongue, catches the hapless prey on the sticky tip of its tongue, and then flips the tongue (together with the prey) back into its mouth. The moor frog completes the process by swallowing the prey whole.

In colder parts of its habitat, the moor frog hibernates during winter, emerging in early March and moving to its breeding grounds. The male croaks to attract a mate. The female, with her excellent sense of hearing, can distinguish a male moor frog's croak from the croaks of other frogs. The female lays from 1,000 to 2,000 eggs, which the male immediately fertilizes. The tiny tadpoles that emerge from the eggs gradually grow up to 1½ inches long before metamorphosing into frogs. Unlike most types of frogs, the adult is actually smaller than the tadpole—approximately one-half the length.

Northern Chorus Frog
Pseudacris triseriata

Length: ¾ to 1½ inches
Diet: mainly insects and spiders
Method of Reproduction: egg layer

Home: eastern and central North America
Order: Frogs and toads
Family: Tree frogs and their relatives

 Fresh Water

Amphibians

North America is home to seven species of chorus frogs. These tree frogs are named for the nighttime sing-alongs performed by the males during breeding season. Northern chorus frogs are an especially hardy species. In early spring, they emerge to sing and mate near ponds and streams—even before winter's ice has completely melted.

The call of the northern chorus frog is an unmistakable high-pitched trill that resembles the sound made by running a fingernail over a fine-tooth comb. Once the males' chorus has attracted a number of females, the frogs slip into the water. Each male grasps a female just beneath her arms. She then lays a mass of jellylike eggs in the water as he fertilizes them. The eggs hatch into fishlike tadpoles, which mature into frogs by the end of the summer. Northern chorus frogs are often heard but seldom seen, because they immediately dive into the water at the least sign of danger. To catch a glimpse of this exceptionally handsome tree frog, one must patiently sit (silent and motionless) until the frog emerges from hiding. This species is distinguished by its greenish-gray to brown skin and three black stripes down the back. There is also a dark strip that runs through each eye and a white "mustache" on the upper lip. Like all tree frogs, the northern chorus species has rounded toe tips that help it cling to wet vegetation.

Ornate Horned Frog
Ceratophrys ornata

Diet: small amphibians, mammals, and other animals
Method of Reproduction: egg layer

Length: 3½ to 5 inches
Home: South America
Order: Frogs and toads
Family: Leptodactylid frogs

 Rainforests

 Amphibians

© KEVIN SCHAFER / CORBIS

Most frogs are timid creatures. They disappear at the slightest sign of danger. But not the ornate horned frog! It could be called the fighter frog because it is an aggressive bully! The ornate horned frog isn't afraid to attack larger animals, and it's even been known to bite the heads of grazing horses.

The ornate horned frog has a big head and a large, heavy body. If you were to look this creature straight in the eyes, it would look as if it were smiling. It has a very wide mouth and extremely strong jaws. It also has the ability to take in lots of air and puff itself up. This makes it look even bigger and scarier. The frog gets its name from the flap of skin on each upper eyelid.

This structure looks like a little horn, but it is not hard or sharp. Its purpose is unknown.

Ornate horned frogs usually live among low-lying plants on damp forest floors. Their coloring is good camouflage, blending into the background and hiding the frogs from prey and predators. Often the frogs will lie under leaves or moss. Only the top of the head and the large, protruding eyes are visible. Ornate horned frogs are always alert, listening to the forest sounds and watching for any signs of movement.

At mating time, ornate horned frogs travel to ponds in the forest. After courting, the females release their eggs into the water, and the males fertilize the eggs.

Paradox Frog
Pseudis paradoxa

Length: 2¾ inches
Length of the Tadpole: 9¾ inches
Method of Reproduction: egg layer

Diet: insects and spiders
Home: eastern South America
Order: Frogs
Family: Pseudids

 Fresh Water

 Amphibians

© TOM MCHUGH / PHOTO RESEARCHERS

A paradox is something that seems contrary to common sense. The paradox frog is so named because, contrary to the way nature usually works, its young tadpoles are larger than the adult frogs. The paradox frog is unusual in other ways as well. Unlike most frogs, this species spends little time on land. And it won't come out of the water at all during the day. But if you are walking through the South American jungle on a dark, rainy night, you might see lots of adult paradox frogs. They would be hopping through the wet underbrush in search of new ponds.

Both adult paradox frogs and their oversized tadpoles spend their days hidden in mats of floating plants. The mats contain plenty of insects for the adult frogs and lots of tender leaves for the tadpoles. The mats also provide good hiding places. And there is good reason to hide! In South America, many ponds contain piranhas and other meat-eating fish that would quickly make a meal out of an unsuspecting frog.

Luckily, paradox tadpoles are exceptional swimmers and can often outrace their enemies. Their bodies are flattened from side to side, with long fins that extend from head to tail. In fact, they look more like fish than like other tadpoles. They swim like fish, too, by wiggling their entire bodies. If you picked up a paradox tadpole, you would quickly realize it was no fish. It would feel like a squishy blob of Jell-O.

Pickerel Frog
Rana palustris

Diet: insects, spiders, and crustaceans
Method of Reproduction: egg layer

Length: 1¾ to 3 inches
Home: eastern North America
Order: Frogs and toads
Family: True frogs

 Fresh Water

 Amphibians

© JOE MCDONALD / CORBIS

The pickerel frog is a meadow frog found throughout much of the eastern United States and Nova Scotia, Canada. It greatly resembles the more familiar leopard frog, except that the dark splotches on the pickerel's body are larger and squarer.

A pickerel frog's belly and inner legs are bright yellow or orange. This vivid coloration often serves as a warning to predators: glands in the pickerel's skin produce a substance that tastes horrible and is poisonous! Most predators quickly spit out the frog and remember to avoid any frog with the same bright colors. The pickerel's secretions may also discourage other frog species from invading its territory. In fact, the poisonous substance will eventually kill any frog that shares a terrarium with the pickerel.

Like many frogs the pickerel is active at night. It announces its presence with a steady, low-pitched croak. It also makes a rumbling sound underwater.

These frogs mate in early spring in slow-moving streams, swamps, or wet meadows. At that time the arms and thumbs of the male swell, enabling him to easily grasp a mate. The female lays masses of eggs and attaches them to underwater plants. The eggs hatch within a month, and the tadpoles mature into frogs by fall. In October, pickerels dig themselves into the mud, where they hibernate until early spring.

Pig Frog
Rana grylio

Diet: insects and other invertebrates, small fish, frogs, and snakes
Number of Eggs: 8,000 to 15,000

Length: 3¼ to 5½ inches
Home: southeastern United States
Order: Frogs and toads
Family: True frogs

Fresh Water

Amphibians

© KARL H. SWITAK / PHOTO RESEARCHERS

The pig frog is named for the gruntlike call made by the males, usually while they float in the water. While other types of frogs call only during mating season or only at night, the pig frog grunts and barks year-round, day and night. But it makes noise only when the temperature is above 70° F. Sometimes groups of pig frogs chime together as a chorus. The sound, some say, is like that of a herd of pigs.

Pig frogs are quite remarkable for their ability to survive in salt water, though they usually live in freshwater marshes. They hardly ever crawl out onto land. Pig frogs prefer to live among thick clumps of water lilies or other aquatic plants. There they can both hide from their predators and find many of their favorite foods—such as crawfish, insects, and snakes. Humidity is an important factor in the pig frog's life. If the creature is not moist enough, it will not eat, look for a partner, or mate.

Many people think that pig-frog legs are tastier than chicken. In the southern United States, people catch pig frogs at night. Frog hunters will quietly row a boat into a marsh and then startle the frogs with the beam of a flashlight. Nearly paralyzed by the light, the pig frogs are easy to catch. Pig-frog hunting is so popular in Louisiana that the state has laws limiting where and when people can catch the tasty animal.

Red-legged Frog
Rana aurora

Length: 2 to 5½ inches
Diet: insects and other small invertebrates
Method of Reproduction: egg layer

Home: Vancouver Island and the West Coast of North America
Order: Frogs and toads
Family: True frogs

 Fresh Water

 Amphibians

© ERWIN & PEGGY BAUER / BRUCE COLEMAN INC.

The red-legged frog is recognized by its slim waist, long legs, and pointed, partly webbed toes. The frog is either reddish brown or gray with many dark spots and blotches. Its underside is yellow, and its back legs and lower belly are light red. The call of the red-legged frog is a low-pitched growl. Each note is long (two or three seconds), but not very loud.

Despite its camouflage coloration, the frog is a familiar sight in its range. It is considerably more active during the day than are other frogs. Red-legged frogs are most common in the damp woods of Vancouver Island and in the coastal rainforests of British Columbia, Washington, and Oregon. The California red-legged frog,

a subspecies, is distinguished by the light "bull's-eye" at the center of its dark spots.

Red-legged frogs mate between January and March. Those in the northern (cooler) part of their range mate later than those in the southern (warmer) part. Regardless of the region, breeding lasts just a few days. During this time, all the adult red-legged frogs gather at the edges of ponds and lakes. The male has especially large arms and fat thumbs, which he uses to grip a female tightly around the chest. As the female sheds large masses of eggs, her mate fertilizes them. The largest, most vocal males mate with many females before the breeding season ends.

Strawberry Poison Dart Frog
Dendrobates pumilio

Length: 1 to 2 inches
Weight: 1 to 2 ounces
Diet: insects
Number of Eggs: 2 to 20

Home: Central and South America
Order: Frogs and toads
Family: Tree frogs

 Forests and Mountains

 Amphibians

© DAVID A. NORTHCOTT / CORBIS

South American Indians use the strong poison produced by the strawberry poison dart frog to coat the tips of their arrows. First the Indians carefully kill the frog by piercing it with a long stick. Then they roast the skewered frog over a fire, much like a marshmallow. As the frog's flesh roasts, it begins to drip poison, which the Indians catch in a jar. They ferment this deadly brew until it is very potent. Then the Indian hunters dip their arrows in the mixture and allow the poison to dry on the tips. A monkey or a bird struck by one of these arrows will be paralyzed almost instantly and drop to the ground.

Most poisonous frogs have bright colors that warn predators that they are dangerous to eat. Oddly enough, the strawberry poison dart frog is dark and very hard to see in the shadowy rainforest. Yet this species has eight times more poison in its skin than more-colorful poison dart frogs.

During the breeding season, male strawberry poison dart frogs are walking nurseries for their young. After mating, the female attaches her eggs to the skin on the male's back. There they remain, even after hatching into tadpoles. As the tadpoles grow, the father must find ever larger holes in which to hide from predators. Eventually he immerses himself in water, and the young swim away.

Arctic Fulmar
Fulmarus glacialis

Length: about 18 inches
Weight: about 20 ounces
Diet: squid, jellyfish,
  crustaceans, and garbage
Number of Eggs: 1

Home: northern oceans
Order: Tubenoses
Family: Typical tubenoses
Subfamily: Fulmars

 Oceans and
Shores

 Birds

© GEORGE MCCARTHY / CORBIS

The arctic fulmar looks like a large, chubby seagull. But a closer look at the top of its beak reveals a "tube nose." The bird is a member of the tubenose family, a group of marine birds with large, tubular nostrils and a keen sense of smell. Arctic fulmars can also be recognized by the way they glide in a zigzag pattern close to the surface of the ocean waves.

These birds swim high on the water and look like big, bobbing corks. Because they are so buoyant, they seldom dive for food. Instead, they sit on the water, scooping up plankton and other small marine animals from the surface. Arctic fulmars have learned to scavenge after commercial fishing fleets. They follow the boats, eating garbage tossed overboard. Thanks to this source of food, fulmars have increased in number.

Male and female fulmars look very similar, except that the male has a larger bill and stockier body. Mated pairs often stay together for life, returning to the same nesting site year after year. They build a simple nest on a rock scrape or on the small, grassy shelf of a steep cliff. If the nest is on solid rock, the birds cushion its bottom with fine, soft materials such as lichen or moss. The parents warm their thick-shelled, 3-inch egg for nearly two months. When it finally hatches, the young chick matures slowly, drinking a rich oil that the parents produce from their stomach.

Gaur
Bos gaurus

Length: 8 to 11 feet
Weight: 1,400 to 2,200 pounds
Height at the Shoulders: 5½ to 7 feet
Diet: grasses and leaves
Number of Young: 1

Home: India and Southeast Asia
Order: Even-toed ungulates
Family: Oxen
Subfamily: Wild cattle

Forests and Mountains

Mammals

© W. PERRY CONWAY / CORBIS

The gaur is the world's largest wild ox. And it's not an animal you'd want to upset! For the most part, the gaur is a peaceful creature. But when injured or scared, it will charge at high speeds, pounding the ground with both front legs at the same time. Despite its huge size, the gaur can also jump and has been known to hurdle fences. Yet the gaur's speed and bulk are not enough to protect it against all predators. It is hunted by tigers as well as by humans.

Gaur live in herds of 8 to 11 individuals. Typically, these groups are made up of several females and their young, led by one adult male. While the male jealously defends his group, he seldom fights with other males. Instead, males have a strict pecking order based almost entirely on size. Smaller males will seldom bother larger ones.

Humans have taken a great interest in the gaur. In eastern India and Burma, villagers raise a tame variety of gaur they call a gayal. In the United States, researchers have tried to breed gaur with cattle, hoping to produce a new type of livestock with lots of meat. These "gaur-cows" have not yet become popular. As sad as it sounds, such domestication and interbreeding may be the gaur's only hope of survival. In the wild, it is found only in small, widely scattered groups. It has been devastated by hunting, the destruction of its home, and by disease spread by domestic cattle.

Gavial
Gavialis gangeticus

Length: up to 23 feet
Diet: fish and frogs
Number of Eggs: up to 40
Method of Reproduction: egg
    layer

Home: India, Nepal, Pakistan,
    Bhutan, and Bangladesh
Order: Crocodiles
Family: Gavials

 Fresh Water

Reptiles

Endangered
Animals

© MICHAEL & PATRICIA FOGDEN / CORBIS

The gavial gets its name from the Hindi word *ghariyāl*. A *ghariyāl* is a long clay pot shaped much like the tip of this crocodile's snout. All crocodiles have long snouts, which is how you can tell them apart from their cousins, the alligators. Alligator snouts are short and wide. Unlike other crocodiles, the gavial does not travel well on solid land. Its legs are short, spindly, and weak. When the gavial crawls out of the water, it cannot even walk properly. It moves with a side-to-side motion called a "belly slide."

In the water the gavial is a speedster. It uses its strong tail as a whiplike propeller. Nature has also given this fearsome predator an impressive set of teeth. You don't have to worry about human-eating gavials,

though. They seldom attack anything larger than fish.

In reality, the gavial has much more to fear from humans than we do from them. For years the gavial was safe in its watery home because the Hindu people felt it belonged to their god Vishnu. But foreigners who came to the Hindu lands of Asia hunted the gavial for its skin. The gavial has also been crowded out of its home by those who needed more room for their towns and villages. By 1970 fewer than 500 gavials were left alive. Fortunately, the Indian and Nepalese governments have begun a program to breed these rare crocodiles in captivity. There are now more than 3,000 gavials—all of them protected by law.

False Gavial
Tomistoma schlegeli

Length: 13 feet or more
Diet: fish and other small vertebrates
Method of Reproduction: egg layer

Home: Thailand, Malaysia, and Indonesia
Order: Crocodilians
Family: Crocodiles

 Fresh Water

Reptiles

© MARK NEWMAN / PHOTO RESEARCHERS

The false gavial—also called the false gharial—lives in swamps, lakes, and rivers, where it swims or floats on the surface. It feeds mainly on fish, but is not too fussy when it comes to food: it also will make a meal of frogs, snakes, birds, and small mammals. Despite its large size and slow movements, the false gavial really comes to life when it spots potential prey. This crocodile is so agile that it can leap into the air and catch birds and bats in midflight!

Although the false gavial looks less than attractive to us, its appearance is a sign that it is well adapted for its watery life. Its body is covered with scales that protect it from attacks by enemies. Its eyes are on top of its head, a feature that allows the gavial to peer along the water's surface and edge while it is almost completely underwater, much like a submarine raising its periscope. The false gavial can also breathe in this position because its nostrils are high on the top of its snout. When it goes underwater, the nostrils close up tightly, and the eyes are protected by a special transparent eyelid.

When it is time to lay her eggs, the female false gavial uses leaves and other vegetation to build a large nest on land. After laying the eggs, she covers them with this vegetation. The rotting plant material produces heat and serves as a natural incubator, warming the eggs.

Dorcas Gazelle
Gazella dorcas

Length: 3½ to 4 feet
Height at the Shoulder: 1¾ to 2 feet
Weight: 33 to 44 pounds
Diet: grasses, herbs, flowers, and succulents

Number of Young: 1 or 2
Home: northern Africa and Middle East
Order: Even-toed hoofed mammals
Family: Bovines

 Deserts

Mammals

BRUCE COLEMAN INC.

? Endangered Animals

Most people have seen gazelles on TV nature shows or at zoos. The dorcas gazelle is the gazelle species most often kept in zoos. But in the wild, it has all but disappeared. Once common throughout Africa's Sahara and Arabian deserts, the dorcas gazelle has recently become victim to severe overhunting and destruction of its environment. Today many races, or subspecies, of this gazelle are in danger of extinction. Among the most endangered are the Saudi Arabian gazelle (*G. d. saudiya*), the Moroccan gazelle (*G. d. massaesyla*), and Pelzelni's gazelle (*G. d. pelzelni*) of Somalia.

Despite the animal's small size and gentle appearance, the male can be quarrelsome and territorial. As a full-grown buck, he marks the boundaries of his "property" with spots of urine and piles of dung. Older bucks are known to attack other male gazelles, zebras, and any creatures that dare to trespass. However, females are always welcome. An established buck may keep up to 40 does in his "harem." Young males are more social and form large male-female herds. Members of the herd are ever wary of danger and warn one another with a ducklike "quack" made through the nose.

Over the years the dorcas gazelle has adapted well to life in the sandy desert. It needs little water and gets most of its moisture from succulent plants and other vegetation.

Blue-tailed Day Gecko
Phelsuma cepediana

Length: 4½ to 5½ inches
Diet: mainly insects
Method of Reproduction: egg
layer

Home: Indian Ocean islands of
Mauritius and Réunion
Order: Lizards and snakes
Family: Geckos

 Rainforests

 Reptiles

Some animals live all over the world and in a variety of habitats. But the blue-tailed day gecko lives naturally only in rainforests, and then only in the rainforests of two small islands in the Indian Ocean. There it spends almost all of its time in trees, seldom moving to the ground. The "blue tail" is active only during the day, when it moves slowly along leaves and branches, looking for insects to eat. As soon as it senses danger, it runs away and hides.

The blue-tailed day gecko is an attractive lizard with a blue or green back and many red spots and other markings. Like a chameleon, it is able to change the color of its skin, which helps to camouflage it.

This reptile runs up and down tree trunks with ease thanks to a special adaptation: tiny suction cups on the undersides of its toes. As the gecko moves, these cups stick to the surface, preventing the animal from falling. When a gecko lifts its foot, it begins by slowly bending back the tip of its toes. It "peels" the foot off the surface, beginning with the toes. When the gecko puts its foot down, the process is reversed. The center of the foot touches the surface first, the toes next, and finally the toe tips.

During the mating season, males call loudly to attract females. After mating, a female lays two or three eggs in a protected spot under the bark of a tree.

Gliding Gecko
Ptychozoon lionotum

Length: 4½ to 6 inches
Diet: insects and spiders
Number of Eggs: 2

Home: Southeast Asia
Order: Lizards and snakes
Family: Geckos

  Rainforests

Reptiles

Many geckos have a thin fringe of skin along their sides. In the gliding gecko, this skin flap developed into something quite remarkable. On each side of the lizard's trunk, a wide fold of skin stretches half the width of its body. Several narrower flaps run along its head and back legs. For a long time, scientists didn't know what to make of these membranes. Then someone dropped a gecko from a height of 20 feet. The animal stiffly spread its legs and tail, and used the membranes to "fly" expertly to the ground. The gliding gecko is further equipped for flight with broad, webbed feet and a flat, fringed tail. Appropriately, the species's scientific name, *Ptychozoon*, means "fold animal."

Gliding geckos never purposefully leave the trees. Rather, they glide from branch to branch. They are most active after sunset when they hunt for insects and spiders. When resting on a tree trunk or branch, the gecko folds its loose skin along its body. Its dull coloration is excellent camouflage.

Many species of gecko can be seen—and heard—throughout the warmer regions of the world. Geckos are the only reptiles with true voices, and the name "gecko" is an imitation of their call. Geckos are also noted for their "suction cup" feet. Rows of tiny, sticky disks on their toes enable this reptile to climb straight up tree trunks and walls, and even to cling upside down on a ceiling.

Madagascar Gecko
Phelsuma madagascariensis

Length: up to 10 inches
Diet: mainly insects
Method of Reproduction: egg layer

Home: Madagascar and nearby islands
Order: Lizards and snakes
Family: Geckos

 Forests and Mountains

 Reptiles

© KIM TAYLOR / BRUCE COLEMAN INC.

The Madagascar gecko is a spectacular-looking animal—for a lizard, that is. Although most geckos are a very dull color, this one is a brilliant emerald green, with bright-red spots on its back. This color scheme is practical as well as dazzling; the green blends with the leaves in the gecko's surroundings, hiding the lizard from hungry falcons and other enemies.

Another unusual protective adaptation of the Madagascar gecko is its "falling trick." When it senses danger, the gecko will suddenly fall off the branch on which it is sitting. It lands feet first among leaves on the ground and is completely hidden.

This lizard spends most of its time in trees, although it also likes to visit balconies on people's houses. Geckos have special microscopic suction disks on the underside of their toes. These disks help them climb, making it easy to cling to branches, tree trunks, and other surfaces. When the gecko wants to lift a foot, it must "peel" the foot off the surface—first bending back the tips of its toes, then the rest of its toes, and finally the center of its foot. When the gecko puts its foot back down, this process is reversed.

Madagascar geckos are active during the daytime. Insects make up most of their diet, but they also enjoy desserts, treating themselves to sugary plant nectar and sweet fruits such as bananas.

Northern Leaf-tailed Gecko
Phyllurus cornutus

Length: 6 to 9 inches
Diet: mainly insects and spiders
Number of Eggs: 2

Home: northeastern Australia
Order: Lizards and snakes
Family: Geckos

 Rainforests

Reptiles

© MICHAEL FOGDEN / BRUCE COLEMAN INC.

The northern leaf-tailed gecko is a strange-looking lizard. Its broad, leaf-shaped tail is the widest part of its body. The creature's triangular head is almost as big. In comparison, the rest of the gecko's body looks puny. From snout to tail tip, this creature is flat as a pancake and covered with long, pointed scales. All in all, the gecko resembles a piece of bark or a dried-out leaf. The lizard's drab, blotchy coloring completes its camouflage. Virtually invisible to enemies, it successfully hides from large predatory birds and snakes.

The northern leaf-tailed gecko lives in a narrow region of coastal rainforest and in an adjoining strip of dry woodland in northeastern Australia. During the day, it sleeps hidden beneath loose strips of bark or inside a tree hole. At night the gecko emerges, hunting for spiders and insects. Crawling on spindly legs, it circles large tree trunks and shinnies up small saplings in search of prey. Like most geckos, this species has tiny suction cups on the bottom of its toe pads. These sticky toes allow the gecko to walk up slick, vertical surfaces and along the undersides of branches without falling off.

Northern leaf-tailed geckos have become less common over the past century. Human development and the introduction of livestock have destroyed much of the species's natural habitat.

Silvery Gibbon (Moloch)
Hylobates lar moloch

Length of the Body: 1½ to 2 feet
Weight: 11 to 13 pounds
Diet: mainly fruits; also leaves

Number of Young: 1; rarely 2
Home: western Java
Order: Primates
Family: Gibbons

 Rainforests

 Mammals

Endangered Animals

© ART WOLFE / PHOTO RESEARCHERS

The moloch, or silvery gibbon, teeters on the brink of extinction. Although all gibbons of Southeast Asia are endangered, this small, gentle species may be in the greatest peril. Its natural habitat is tiny—only the western half of the island of Java. And humans have cut down large portions of the Javan rainforest in recent years. These factors have forced the moloch to compete for dwindling space with more-aggressive apes.

Tailless, long-limbed, and slender, this graceful gibbon has long silver-gray fur. The flattened fur atop its head and on its belly is darkest. Even when hidden in the treetops, molochs can be distinguished from other gibbons by their song. Each gibbon species

has a unique voice and melody. Like all gibbons, the moloch swings effortlessly hand over hand through the trees. When resting, it simply dangles by one arm.

This primate lives in small, "nuclear" families, consisting of a father, mother, and several youngsters of various ages. Each morning the family greets the dawn with a chorus of lively calls. With these songs, they proclaim their territory to surrounding gibbon groups. Molochs seldom fight with family members. When one gibbon finds a tasty fruit, it is likely to pass the treat around so everyone can have a bite. At six or seven years, young molochs leave their parents' group and establish families of their own.

White-cheeked Gibbon
Hylobates concolor

Length of the Body: 1½ to 2 feet
Weight: 13 to 15½ pounds
Diet: fruits, leaves, flowers, and insects

Number of Young: 1
Home: Southeast Asia
Order: Primates
Family: Gibbons

 Rainforests

 Mammals

 Endangered Animals

© E. R. DEGGINGER / COLOR PIC, INC.

When standing upright, the lanky, tailless gibbon looks almost human. Perhaps the most striking difference is the gibbon's amazingly long, strong arms. The gibbon is the only creature in the world that can travel through the trees by swinging hand over hand without ever using its feet. It can leap several yards from one tree to the next and can swing around a tree trunk as if the trunk were a greased pole.

So strong are the gibbon's arms that it seldom tires of "hanging out." Just as a human rests on his or her feet, a gibbon can effortlessly hang from a tree branch by one or both arms, often for long stretches of time. Importantly, the gibbon's long arms give it a very long reach. It can stretch out to pick the tastiest fruits and blossoms off the tips of the thinnest branches.

There are five different species of gibbon, all about the same size, all living in Southeast Asia, and all in danger of extinction. The white-cheeked, or crested, gibbon is particularly endangered. It survives only in small, isolated groups, mainly on the island of Hainan and in the country of Vietnam.

Male white-cheeked gibbons are pure black, except for light-colored sideburns. Females of this species have light body fur, with a dark crest on their head. The babies are generally dark like their father, but may not have his light-colored cheeks.

Reticulated Giraffe
Giraffa camelopardalis reticulata

Length: 13 to 15 feet
Height: up to 16 feet
Diet: leaves and twigs of trees, especially acacias
Number of Young: usually 1

Home: eastern Africa
Order: Even-toed hoofed mammals
Family: Giraffes and okapis

 Grasslands

 Mammals

© JOE MCDONALD / CORBIS

A giraffe is easily recognizable by its amazingly long neck, which enables it to feed on the leaves of tall trees. Despite its length, however, a giraffe's neck has only seven bones in the skeleton—the same number of bones as in a human neck!

There are eight subspecies of giraffes, which differ in color, markings, and the number of horns. The reticulated giraffe is named for its coat, with its network (reticulation) of light lines enclosing large dark brown spots. A stubby mane runs down the back of its neck, and its tail ends in a tuft of long hair.

Adult male giraffes are called bulls; the females, which are smaller, are called cows. The female giraffe is pregnant for about 15 months, and she gives birth standing up. This means that a newborn giraffe's first experience is falling to the ground from a height of more than six feet! The baby is sturdy, however, and attempts to stand soon after birth.

Giraffes are born big. A newborn male may be 6 feet tall and weigh more than 200 pounds; females weigh about half as much. These animals can live up to 25 years, although few die of old age. Many calves die during the first few months of life, falling prey either to disease or to such enemies as lions. Those giraffes that do reach old age make easy prey as well. A healthy adult giraffe has almost no natural enemies.

Yellow-bellied Glider
Petaurus australis

Length of the Body: about 12 inches
Length of the Tail: 16 to 19 inches
Diet: nectar, pollen, tree sap, and insects

Weight: 16 to 25 pounds
Number of Young: 1
Home: southeastern Australia
Order: Marsupials
Family: Phalangers

 Forests and Mountains

Mammals

© A.N.T. / NHPA

The yellow-bellied glider is a tree-dwelling marsupial (pouched) mammal, named for the golden fur on the underside of its dark body. The glider is about the size of a rabbit, but much lighter in weight. When it leaps from a perch, it stretches out its limbs to extend two gliding membranes. In this way the creature can "fly" great distances from one tree to another. To steer, it uses its exceptionally long tail.

"Yellowbellies" live in the warm, humid eucalyptus forests of southeastern Australia. Like most gliders, they are active at night. Although they catch some insects, the gliders are primarily vegetarians. They are especially fond of sweet nectar, pollen, and eucalyptus sap. They tap into eucalyptus trees by biting numerous holes in the bark.

These agile creatures live in small family groups. In the southernmost part of their range, each mated pair lives with their young offspring. Farther north, yellowbellies form harems in which one male lives with as many as five females and their young. Each family shares a large territory (50 to 125 acres), which it establishes with strongly scented markings and a considerable amount of screeching. Family members also mark each other with special odors. Unfortunately, yellow-bellied gliders are growing quite rare because people continue to cut down Australia's eucalyptus forests, areas vital to the survival of the gliders and many other creatures.

Wild Goat
Capra aegagrus

Length: 4 to 5⅓ feet
Height at the Shoulder: 2⅓ to 3⅓ feet
Weight: 55 to 88 pounds
Diet: mainly grasses and herbs
Number of Young: 1 or 2

Home: Middle East
Order: Even-toed hoofed mammals
Family: Bovines
Subfamily: Sheep and goats

 Forests and Mountains

Mammals

© KENNETH W. FINK / PHOTO RESEARCHERS

? Endangered Animals

The ancestors of our farm goats still roam the high cliffs and mountains of the Middle East. But centuries of hunting have brought the wild goat to the brink of extinction. A few small groups survive in high mountains, where it is difficult for humans to reach them. But the wild goat has other enemies as well. Its young are often killed by wolves, foxes, and hyenas. And wild goat herds must compete for food with domestic goats.

Recently naturalists imported a herd of wild goats to the Florida Mountains of New Mexico. From an original population of 30 bucks (males) and 43 does (females), the herd now numbers more than 1,000.

The wild goat is known for its sturdy, muscular body. A buck grows dramatic,

sickle-shaped horns up to 4½ feet in length. The doe also grows horns, but hers are usually less than a foot long. A newborn wild goat enters the world weighing only 4 to 8 pounds. But it is soon strong enough to leap after its mother atop steep cliffs.

The wild goat is also called a bezoar, after the "bezoar stones" found in its stomach. Superstitious people believed that these stones were magical and could cure disease. In truth, bezoars are simply round clumps of undigested hair, which the goat licks from its coat. Over time, these hair balls compress in the goat's stomach until they are as hard and smooth as stone.

Magpie Goose
Anseranas semipalmata

Length: 30 to 35 inches
Weight: about 4½ pounds
Diet: grain and other plant matter
Number of Eggs: 5 to 14

Home: Australia
Order: Ducks and screamers
Family: Swans, geese, and ducks

 Fresh Water

Birds

© ERIC & DAVID HOSKING / CORBIS

The magpie goose's Latin genus name, *Anseranas*, means "duck-goose." But in reality, this bird is neither a true duck nor a true goose. Unlike other ducks and geese, the magpie goose's feet are only partly webbed. Also, the bird has a long hind toe, something not seen in any other species of duck or goose.

Scientists greatly value the magpie goose for its unusual characteristics, and they loudly protested when Australia's rice farmers began shooting thousands of these birds each season. But the farmers had a problem: the geese grazed and nested on flooded rice fields. Not only did they eat the farmers' crop, but they also trampled down the rice plants when they built their large nests. Working together the scientists and farmers finally solved the problem. They discovered that magpie geese nested only on flooded rice fields with a certain depth of water. Today Australian rice farmers partly drain their fields during the goose's breeding season. This has forced the bird to return to the lagoons, its natural habitat.

Magpie geese are named for their handsome black-and-white markings, which resemble those of the familiar magpie of Europe. They are very social birds that travel and nest in huge flocks, sometimes numbering several thousand. Although a breeding pair usually stays together for life, the male may keep two mates.

Common Goral
Nemorhaedus goral

Length of the Body: about 4 feet
Length of the Tail: about 7 inches
Height at the Shoulder: about 2½ feet
Weight: 75 to 90 pounds

Diet: grasses, leaves, twigs, and nuts
Number of Young: 1; rarely 2
Home: central Asia
Order: Even-toed hoofed mammals
Family: Bovines

 Forests and Mountains

Mammals

© TOM MCHUGH / PHOTO RESEARCHERS

The goral is an antelope that closely resembles a domestic goat. It is related to the chamois of Europe and the Rocky Mountain goat of North America. Like its cousins the goral nimbly and fearlessly runs across steep, rocky mountainsides.

For centuries the goral escaped its enemies by fleeing onto tall rocks. This kept the animal out of the reach of wolves and wild cats. When humans arrived with guns, hunters shot great numbers of gorals for their warm fur and tasty meat. Even more were killed simply for their horns and organs, which the Chinese used in folk medicines. Today the goral's population is greatly reduced. The survivors generally live in wilderness areas not frequented by people.

In the early morning and late afternoon, gorals emerge from their nighttime hiding places in the rocks. They graze primarily on grasses and supplement their diet with tender branches and acorns. Along the Asian-Pacific coast, gorals make their way to the shore to eat seaweed and drink seawater. This provides salt and other minerals important to their health.

Gorals live in family groups of 15 to 30 animals. The members seldom gather in one place, but peacefully share a wide area. To mark their boundaries, bucks in the group spray urine and leave piles of dung. They also leave behind a smelly substance by rubbing their head against rocks and trees.

Striped Gourami
Colisa fasciata

Length: about 5 inches
Diet: plant and animal matter
Number of Eggs: 600 to 1,000
Home: Southeast Asia

Order: Perchlike fishes
Family: Labyrinth fishes
Subfamily: Gouramis

 Fresh Water

 Fish

© HANS REINHARD / BRUCE COLEMAN INC.

The beautiful striped gourami has 14 or more colorful bands across its body. You can tell the sexes apart by looking for two bars under the fish's chin. The male's chin stripes are darker and more distinct than the female's. He also tends to be redder. When kept as pets, striped gourami are most brilliant when their water is warm, between 77 and 79 degrees Fahrenheit.

Many types of gourami, including this species, have long, threadlike fins on either side of their body. These delicate filaments are very sensitive. Gourami use them, not only as feelers, but also to smell and taste the water. This may help the gourami find mates, as well as avoid enemies.

People who keep striped gourami in aquariums know to quickly remove the female after she spawns. If given the chance, she readily eats her own eggs. It is the male striped gourami who has the more nurturing nature. He tries to build a bubble nest for the eggs and newly hatched young, called fry. But his best efforts are often no more than a mouthful of bubbles scattered across the top of the tank. The eggs seldom stay in the poorly constructed nest and often float to the top of the tank. The father gourami also sprays the eggs with mouthfuls of sand just before they hatch. Even after the fry have hatched, the father follows them about the tank, squirting them with air bubbles and sand.

Blue-winged Wasteland Grasshopper
Oedipoda caerulescens

Length: ⅞ to 1⅛ inches
Wingspan: about 2¼ inches
Method of Reproduction: egg layer
Home: Europe, northern Africa, and southwest Asia

Diet: plants
Order: Grasshoppers and their relatives
Family: Short-horned grasshoppers

 Grasslands

 Arthropods

© DIETMAR NILL / NATURE PICTURE LIBRARY

The blue-winged wasteland grasshopper displays its light blue back wings in flight. In some individuals, each blue wing is lightly dusted in yellow or pink and marked by a black band. To confuse predators, the grasshopper quickly folds and hides its colorful wings when it lands. This makes the insect seem to disappear; its body is a drab brown or gray, much like the rocks and dirt on which it lives. When camouflage alone does not fool an enemy, the grasshopper uses its mighty jaws. Many curious children and insect collectors have discovered this insect's painful bite!

As a group, locusts and grasshoppers are infamous for their destructive appetites. The wasteland grasshopper is an exception. Instead of attacking crops, it stays in the wilderness. Its habitats include the heaths, rocky meadows, dry hillsides, and sandpits of southern and Central Europe.

When temperatures soar in August, the female wasteland grasshopper searches for a place to lay her eggs. She must find a clear patch of dirt into which she can squeeze her long abdomen. As she pushes her body into the ground, she squirts out fertilized eggs mixed with a frothy liquid. The froth stiffens into a protective egg pod inside the soil. After she has laid her eggs, the female carefully pats down the soil with her feet. This entire process takes about an hour.

Green Valley Grasshopper
Schistocerca shoshone

Length: 1½ to 2½ inches
Length of the Wing: 1¼ to 2¼ inches
Diet: leaves of many kinds of plants
Method of Reproduction: egg layer

Home: Mexico and western United States
Order: Grasshoppers and their relatives
Family: Short-horned grasshoppers

 Grasslands

Arthropods

© R. J. ERWIN / PHOTO RESEARCHERS

The green valley grasshopper is a close relative of the locust that plagued Egypt in stories from the Bible. The Egyptian locust is the most destructive grasshopper in the world. It swarms in Europe, Asia, and Africa, and destroys crops over huge areas. Swarms of green valley grasshoppers also destroy crops, but not to the extent of the dreaded locust.

Normally, green valley grasshoppers live in weeds along roadsides and in other places where plants grow thickly. The leaves provide the grasshoppers with plenty of food as well as hiding places from predators. Grasshoppers are eaten by many birds, reptiles, and amphibians.

Once in a while, when the weather is particularly nice and the food supply plentiful, the population of green valley grasshoppers explodes. So many grasshoppers are born that they eat every edible leaf in the area, causing widespread crop devastation. Then the grasshoppers gather in a swarm and fly away in search of a new home. If they find another place with lots of food, the grasshoppers lay more eggs, and their population swells even more. Once again, after they have eaten all the food in the area, the grasshoppers swarm and move on. Eventually the growing grasshopper population runs out of food and "crashes," leaving only a few survivors.

Greenfinch
Carduelis chloris

Length: about 6 inches
Weight: about 1 ounce
Diet: seeds, thistles, and insects
Number of Eggs: 4 to 6

Home: Europe and northern Africa
Order: Perching birds
Family: Finches

 Forests and Mountains

 Birds

© FRANK BLACKBURN / ECOSCENE / CORBIS

The greenfinch is named for the olive-green feathers of the adult male. The female is a dull gray, but both sport wings edged with yellow. European bird lovers easily recognize this species, even from a distance. As it flies, the greenfinch playfully dips and bobs through the air.

During breeding season, greenfinches catch insects and feed them to their chicks. But most of the year, the bird prefers a diet of small seeds and thistle heads. The greenfinch's bill is especially stout and strong—perfect for cracking open seeds. When not eating, greenfinches live in the treetops. Hidden in the leaves, they fill the air with canarylike twittering.

Greenfinches mate in spring. The female builds a nest in a hedge, bush, or small evergreen tree. She incubates her eggs for about two weeks. The male contributes by bringing food to his mate and their chicks. When the young greenfinches leave the nest, they are all the color of the female. Males develop their bright plumage the following spring.

The greenfinch shares its home range with its close cousin the goldfinch. It is unusual for two very similar species to live in one place without one forcing out the other. These two species coexist because they prefer different nesting sites. The greenfinch lives in low bushes and shrubs, while the goldfinch nests on high tree branches.

Greenshank
Tringa nebularia

Length: about 12 inches
Diet: insects and their larvae, crustaceans, and small fish
Home: Europe, Asia, Africa, and Australia

Number of Eggs: usually 4
Order: Wader and gull-like birds
Family: Sandpipers and their relatives

 Fresh Water

□ Summer ■ Winter

Birds

© NIGEL J. DENNIS / GALLO IMAGES / CORBIS

When a greenshank is hungry, it wades into a lake or river, lowers its long, straight bill into the water, and swings the bill from side to side like a sword. Any animal in the bill's path is swallowed, although the bird is most interested in insects and small crustaceans.

The greenshank lives in marshes and other wetland habitats, both inland and along the coasts. The bird's dark, speckled black-and-white underparts help conceal it from predators. The greenshank is named for its long greenish legs (shanks), which extend beyond the bird's tail in flight. As the greenshank soars above the water, it often calls out a loud "tew tew tew."

When the female, who looks more or less like the male, is ready to reproduce, she builds a nest among grasses and low bushes close to shore. The nest is usually near an easy-to-recognize object, such as a boulder or a log. That way the female will have an easy time finding her nest. After the eggs are laid, the parents take turns incubating them for about 24 days. When the parents change places, they call "chip chip chip!" Baby greenshanks begin to fly when they are about a month old.

Greenshanks migrate with the seasons. They winter in warm tropical and subtropical places. In spring, they fly north to breeding grounds in northern Europe and Asia. Some are even sighted in Alaska.

Double-banded Sand Grouse

Pterocles bicinctus

Length: 10 to 11 inches
Number of Eggs: 2 or 3
Home: dry savannas of southern Africa

Diet: mainly hard seeds
Order: Pigeons, doves, and their relatives
Family: Sand grouse

 Grasslands

 Birds

© BRENDAN RYAN / GALLO IMAGES / CORBIS

For double-banded sand grouse, togetherness is an important way of life. These birds live in large flocks in dry, open areas that are covered with sand and short grass far from rivers or other bodies of water. Each morning, as the sun rises, the flocks fly many miles to special watering holes. During the flight the birds continually twitter to one another. When the sand grouse reach a watering hole, they lower their bills and drink the water without raising their heads. After drinking their fill, the flocks return to their feeding and nesting grounds. In the evening, they again fly to the same watering hole. Each round trip may cover 100 miles—an enormous distance to travel twice a day.

The double-banded sand grouse feeds on seeds it finds on the ground. When it wants to rest, it makes a shallow depression in the ground, settles down, and dusts itself. The dust and the bird's mottled feathers surround the creature, acting as camouflage against enemies.

This bird makes its nest in a depression in the ground, often under a baobab tree. The grouse uses little or no nesting materials; only a few pieces of grass may be placed atop the sand. Both parents incubate the eggs—the female during the day and the male at night. The young are born covered with soft down feathers. Their parents feed them with partly digested food. The young grouse begin to leave the nest soon after they hatch.

Guanaco
Lama guanicoe

Length of the Body: 5 to 6½ feet
Height at the Shoulder: 3 to 4 feet
Weight: 175 to 265 pounds
Diet: mainly grass

Number of Young: 1
Home: Andes Mountains of South America
Order: Even-toed hoofed mammals
Family: Camels

 Grasslands

 Mammals

© GALEN ROWELL / CORBIS

High in South America's Andes Mountains lives the guanaco, a member of the camel family that looks like a cross between a llama and an alpaca. Scientists question exactly what the relationship among these three animals is.

Guanacos move quickly and gracefully over dry grasslands. Their legs are slender but strong, enabling them to run as fast as 35 miles per hour. Guanacos are good swimmers, too. One of their favorite pastimes is lying in the cool water of a swiftly running mountain stream. During dry seasons, guanacos can live for long periods of time without drinking water. They survive only on the water found in the plants they eat.

Guanacos live in small herds. The main herds consist of 5 to 15 females, their young, and a single adult male. Female guanacos give birth every other year. A baby guanaco weighs 20 to 35 pounds at birth and is able to stand and run immediately. When young males are a year old, they are driven out of the family herd to live in bachelor herds until they find mates and start their own families.

The guanaco has a thick coat of fine wool. The coat is longest on the body; it is shorter on the head, neck, and legs. The animal has large eyes and upright ears. Eyes and ears are very important to guanacos because they use them to sense danger. The main enemies of guanacos are people and pumas. In case of danger, guanacos warn one another with a high trilling call.

Common Gudgeon
Gobio gobio

Length: about 6 inches
Diet: insects, worms, plants, and larval fish
Method of Reproduction: scatter eggs and sperm into water

Home: England to central China
Order: Carps and their relatives
Family: Minnows and carps

 Fresh Water

 Fish

© JANE BURTON / BRUCE COLEMAN INC.

Throughout its European home, the common gudgeon is known as an easy fish to catch. In fact, it comes so quickly to a baited hook that the nickname "gudgeon" is sometimes used for a person who is readily fooled or "baited." Most European fishermen throw their gudgeon in a bucket to use to catch larger fish. But in France, gudgeon is prepared as a delicacy in fine restaurants.

The common gudgeon lives along the gravelly bottom of clear, swift-flowing streams. It likes to hide in rocks and crevices, venturing out to dig through the gravel in search of worms and insects. It also nibbles at the leaves and roots of plants growing on the edge of streams.

Male and female gudgeons are hard to tell apart, except during breeding season. At this time the males grow small white "tubercles," or warts, on their head. Gudgeons don't compete for mates or even woo one another with courtship displays. They simply gather in large groups and release their sperm and eggs into the water at the same time.

The common gudgeon has a special sense organ called a "Weberian apparatus," which gives it a primitive sort of sonar. The apparatus is made by four or five fused bones in the fish's back, which carry sound vibrations to the creature's inner ear. Using this sense, the gudgeon can listen for both prey and predators.

Peruvian Guemal
Hippocamelus antisiensis

Length: 4½ to 5½ feet
Weight: 100 to 145 pounds
Number of Young: 1
Home: Andes Mountains of South America

Diet: grasses
Order: Even-toed hoofed animals
Family: Deer

 Forests and Mountains

Mammals

? Endangered Animals

The Peruvian guemal's yellowish gray-brown coat feels rough to the touch, although few people have had the opportunity to pet one. This is because the guemal is critically endangered. Guemals were once found in large herds throughout the Andes Mountains. But people overhunted these small deer for food and pushed them out of their natural homes to make room for cattle. The Peruvian guemal has dwindled to such small numbers that it is considered an endangered species.

Biologists argue about the guemal's personality: some say it is a very shy creature, while others have found it to be extremely friendly, even tame. Perhaps guemals behave differently depending on where they live and their past experience with humans. Because the animals are so rare, scientists have not been able to study enough of them to know for sure.

The small number of Peruvian guemals that have survived spend their summers high in the mountains and move down to the warmer valleys for the winter. They tend to travel and feed in small groups. An older male often joins several mothers with their young. The group grazes on grasses and low-growing plants, and has been seen nibbling by moonlight as well as during the day. Guemals usually mate in June or August—wintertime in Peru. They give birth to one fawn in February or March.

Moustached Guenon
Cercopithecus cephus

Length of the Body: 1⅓ to 2 feet
Length of the Tail: 1½ to 2½ feet
Diet: fruits, flowers, and invertebrates

Weight: 6½ to 14 pounds
Number of Young: 1
Home: western Africa
Order: Primates
Family: Old World monkeys

 Rainforests

 Mammals

© TOM MCHUGH / PHOTO RESEARCHERS

The moustached guenon's (pronounced ´gwe-known) face looks as though it were dipped in blue paint, creating a striking contrast to the monkey's greenish-brown body fur. Blue skin and green fur are unusual in the mammal world. The moustached species is further distinguished from other guenons by a broad white stripe of skin above its upper lip. Completing its costume is a set of bushy white whiskers on either side of the face.

The moustached species is one of the most familiar guenons. Unlike most guenons, which stay hidden in the rainforest's canopy, the moustached variety lives in the lower, more easily viewed branches. Often a moustached guenon family will occupy the "downstairs

apartment" of a tree, while one or more families of crowned guenons live directly above it.

Moustached guenons are especially lively creatures. A typical guenon family includes just one adult male. The family spends its entire day racing from branch to branch. Guenons are quite abundant, largely because they are not bothered by human disturbances. In fact, there are large populations where people have planted oil-palm trees. In these half-wild, half-cultivated areas, the monkey's diet consists almost entirely of the fleshy palm fruit. The oil palm does not grow in the wildest parts of the jungle. There the guenon survives on tender sprouts, young leaves, and flowers.

Set Index